THE
ATHLETIC
ADVANTAGE

10 LESSONS TO BECOMING
A PREMIER ATHLETE

AARON HINES

The Athletic Advantage: 10 Lessons to Becoming A Premier Athlete

Limits of Liability and Disclaimer of Warranty

TESTIMONIALS

"I've worked with many world class trainers and coaches throughout my golf career, and Aaron is by far one of the best! He is a very knowledgeable and personable fitness professional. Not to mention he has one of the healthiest beards I've ever seen!" — Adam Button (Golfer)

"Personal fitness has been a huge part of my life and career. After undergoing a scope on my knee at age 52 getting back into shape was becoming frustrating and I was losing interest. I began working with Aaron and immediately saw results and more importantly my passion for working out was rekindled. Aaron has an outstanding grasp of all fitness and training methods and did a great job of adjusting my workout routines to any physical limitations that I had. More importantly Aaron provided encouragement and humor throughout the process which made the hard work enjoyable. Based upon the 3 months Aaron trained me I would wholeheartedly endorse him to anyone who's willing to put in the hard work." — Bruce Matthews (NFL Hall of Famer)

"Aaron is absolutely phenomenal!!! My daughter had never lifted weights or really worked out. Aaron was very patient with her. They started in February of 2017 and in three months together they transformed her body. She lost around 25lbs and became an athletic young lady. Then in November 2017 she signed for an athletic scholarship. If we hadn't found Aaron then she probably would not have been afforded that opportunity. He is a true professional!!! He strengthens your mind and body in a very safe and efficient manner. He challenges you in different ways but always stays positive. You can't put a price tag on your child's future!!!! Thank you Aaron for your commitment to helping Maggie reach her full potential!!!" —Billy Anderson (Maggie-Cumberland Golf)

"Aaron is the best Physical Trainer in the Middle Tennessee area. If you want to see results fast and also your strength and physical appearance to soar through the roof, he's your guy. He will push you to your best but at the same time he's a laid back and easy guy to talk to and is a great friend. Highly recommend him." —Zach Polisky (University of Tennessee Walk On)

"My 6th grader has been training with Aaron at Premier Performance during the winter break from school. He enjoys working out with Aaron and he was also glad to see some kids from his middle school there too. And I love that he's getting great instruction on proper form while learning how to lift correctly. WIN WIN!" —Sherra Wagner (Little League World Series-2021)

"If you have a son or daughter who is even considering playing colleges sports, you need Mr. Aaron Hines. If it were not for Aaron our son would have continued to try and play through an injury, that may have ended his opportunity to play the sport he loves so much. A trainer needs integrity and knowledge and Aaron understands the muscle mechanics within each sport and centers your training to those specific muscle groups (we found out the hard way, the importance of this). I highly recommend him, especially if college sports are on the horizon. Not to mention, he's one of the kindest guys you'll ever meet." —Jennifer Barina (Shelden UTM Golf)

"I started working with Aaron when I was in 7th grade. Since then he's helped me put on over 35lbs and 25mph of clubhead speed. I moved away from Tennessee to New Hampshire at the start of 2020. We worked around this by doing workouts on Facetime. He worked with the equipment I had; a set of dumbbells, a med ball and a few bands. Even with minimal equipment Aaron helped me win multiple tournaments this year including a state tournament. If you want a plan that's personalized for the best results and someone that is dedicated to get you there then Aaron is the man." —Joshua Phillips (NHIAA Division II Individual State Championship 2020)

"My son Ty started with Aaron almost 5 months ago. I have seen tremendous gains in both his physical appearance and mental toughness. Aaron brings more than just training to him, he brings friendship, support out of the gym at his sports and someone he looks up to. If you are willing to work hard and make sacrifices to obtain personal goals, Premier Performance Training is the place you need to be. In season workouts and off season workouts has been beneficial to Ty and he is excelling at his sports both

10 Lessons to Becoming a Premier Athlete

Football and Baseball. Thank you Aaron for your leadership , support and friendship. —Rob Collins

"My son, Cannon, started with Aaron right before the beginning of Summer. Due to Covid, and our son being a new driver, we took a family friend's recommendation because PPT was so close to home. Well we definitely ended up with more than a convenient gym. We ended up with a solid trainer who will definitely be a part of our son's yearly training. With Cannon being a travel hockey player, his needs differ from most athletes, and Aaron was very knowledgeable in training him the proper way. Cannon was still able to workout with his football buddies, but was able to pay attention to the details that he needed. Another expertise that Aaron has is his ability to push/ motivate his young athletes. Most of his clients are self-motivating/ambitious athletes but he has a way of making them want to give even more. Our son often wants to drop in, during his season, when his team doesn't have planned workouts. Just to get a workout in with Aaron! Like I said earlier, we found Aaron on recommendation and we hope you will take our recommendation and try Premier Performance Training out. I believe you will

THE ATHLETIC ADVANTAGE

be pleased! —Jeff Lentz-(Son Cannon-Janesville Jets NAHL '21/'22)

"Aaron is a fantastic personal and sports trainer!! His knowledge and background in orthopedics provides for safe training. He gears his training to be age, sport and goal specific. My boys are always excited to workout! He is encouraging and provides motivation coupled with training specifically tailored to each of my sons for them to reach their goals and full potential." —Catherine Messer

"In the beginning of August 2019, I needed to get my son with a personal trainer. My son plays baseball, but needed to add strength and weight. I asked around and Aaron Hines was suggested by many people. I contacted Aaron and me and my son met with him. At the first meeting, Aaron asked a lot of questions and tailored the workout and nutritional program to meet my son's needs and goals. Over a 5 month period, my son put on 28 lbs. of muscle. Because of these results, my son made his high school's Varsity baseball team. After baseball is over this Fall, both of my boys will start training with Premier Performance Training. If you want to achieve your workout goals, I would highly recommend contacting Aaron Hines!!!" —Brent Phillps

"Our son Eli had so much respect and admiration for Aaron! Eli always looked forward to his time training with Aaron and felt it was always worth the drive for training. He felt this way because he had so much respect for Aaron's knowledge, patience and encouragement along with his attention to detail for the sport specific training Eli needed in addition to the training during and after recovery of a broken ankle and the results Eli gained. Our family cannot say enough about Aaron Hines and Premier Performance Training! If you are in the Franklin, Nolensville, Brentwood area or within a comfortable driving distance from Franklin and you need a guy with all the right training experience and knowledge for yourself or your young athlete, and you want results, Aaron is your man!

He is a sports specific/needs specific trainer for all levels of athletes-beginning, high school, college and professional. He is excellent with training those of us who want to stay healthy or be healthier, lose weight or recover from a surgery or injury or to get back to our favorite form of exercise or train for an event.

THE ATHLETIC ADVANTAGE

Knowledge, patience, genuine care, experience and RESULTS are what you can expect when training with Aaron Hines!" —Cassy Grow (Eli Grows Mom)

Dedication

To my client and one of the hardest working kids I have ever trained Eli Grow. My hope is that this book will inspire other kids just like you to, "Never Take Anything for Granted."

To my first mentor who took a chance on me while I was in graduate school in Tallahassee, FL—Vince Graham.

ACKNOWLEDGMENTS

This book might not be but one hundred or so pages, but it is packed with 18 years of learning, blood, sweat, tears, and tons of sacrifice. I would like to acknowledge my team of supporters who have stuck with me from the beginning of this journey.

To my wife Amanda for sacrificing a ton of time and energy being married to a first time entrepreneur. It's not easy, but she has been by my side encouraging me to be a better person and business owner each and every day.

To my kids, Stetson and Lincoln, who make life fun and keep me on my toes each and every day. I am constantly driving to provide the best opportunities for each one of them.

THE ATHLETIC ADVANTAGE

To my parents and brothers for always being there and supporting me in whatever I did.

To my friends who have supported me from day one of starting my own business (Jacob Engelman) and to Mr. Collier for letting me tag along to all of the workouts during my Junior and Senior Years of High School. You taught me a ton about working out.

To each and every one of my clients who have sacrificed their time and energy to become a part of Premier Performance Training LLC over the past 5 years. All of your encouragement has helped me push for more things outside of my comfort zone each and every day. You make my job fun and entertaining on a daily basis.

About the Author

Aaron Hines is a husband, father, and entrepreneur. He lives west of Nashville TN in a small town of Bellevue with his wife Amanda and two sons, Lincoln and Stetson. He played all 4 years of High School football and spent two years in College playing offensive and defensive line at Lambuth University. He graduated from the University of Tennessee at Martin with an undergraduate degree in Health and

THE ATHLETIC ADVANTAGE

Human Performance and also has a M.S. in Exercise Physiology from Florida State University.

He owns and operates a fitness facility in Franklin TN, where he helps change the lives of those individuals 45+ who want to lose weight, move pain free, and do things they didn't think were possible.

He also spends a lot of time and energy helping young athletes reach their full potential by teaching them the fundamentals of being a great person and athlete on and off the field.

He was voted one of the Top Personal Trainers in all of Nashville in 2020 and was featured in the Franklin Lifestyle Magazine in 2019.He can be reached at Premierperformancetrainer.com, 615-819-5186, or ahines@premierperformancetrainer.com

Connect with Coach Aaron:

Facebook: @premierperformancetn
Twitter: @thepremierpt
Instagram: @premierperformancetn

A Bonus Gift For You:

As a thank you for reading, The Athletic Advantage, I have put together an exclusive offer just for you. You can access it by scanning the QR Code Below.

TABLE OF CONTENTS

FOREWORD

As a high school and college football coach for over 30 years, I have had the opportunity to coach hundreds if not thousands of young men. My goal has always been to leave a positive mark on each and everyone of them. But ever so often, a young man comes along and you realize they have something special. Sometimes it's their athletic ability and sometimes it's their ability to inspire others. Concerning Aaron, it wasn't his athletic ability, but it was his "mindset" that made an impact on the team and also on me. Aaron was that young man that worked harder and was more committed to his and the team's goals than the average player.

When Aaron first arrived on campus at Lambuth University, he was just one of several fresh faces wanting to play college football. Like many freshmen,

1

he was not very noticeable average height, average weight, just average... except for his Amish style beard. However, it was not long that myself and other coaches noticed the drive and determination of this undersized lineman everyone called Jebediah. He was never one to shy away from a challenge. In our one-on-one drills the upperclassmen were asking, "Who is this freshman that keeps jumping to the front of the line?" I don't know how many one-on-one's Aaron won, but I'll tell you this, "He was always there to compete!"

Aaron stayed with us at Lambuth for a couple of years. And then the realization hit him. The realization that comes to every football player. The one universal fact about football. Your playing days will end. They do for everyone. For many it is in middle school, for many more it is in high school, and for those that make it, it is in college. Aaron realized that it was time for him to attempt something new. Something that would become his career or should I say his passion.

As is common in the coaching profession, I left the university and had a few coaching jobs in a few different locations. Ten years after my stint at

Lambuth University my family and I moved to the Nashville area for another coaching job. One of the first people to reach out to me was Aaron. I soon realized that several of the players I was coaching either knew of Aaron or were being trained by him. Each of them had nothing but great things to say about him. As a coach, I could see the development these athletes were making under his training. However, it was not Aaron's training the players kept talking about. It was how he genuinely cared about them and their success. Aaron would come to our freshman, JV, and varsity games to see the players he was training. It was amazing to see the relationship he had developed with them. And it was heartwarming for an "old ball coach" to see one of his former players doing what he loved and doing it well!

I have known Aaron for close to twenty years now. I have seen his drive, determination, and passion first hand. He is always looking to help someone be a better version of themselves. As a player, I don't know if he realized how much his work ethic and sacrifice benefited his teammates. Oftentimes people work in the shadows and never realize the impact they make on others. Aaron was one of those people.

THE ATHLETIC ADVANTAGE

His coaches always talked about him when the subject of being a good teammate arose.

It is because of these examples, I can honestly say that if Aaron believes it can happen and wants it to happen, I'll put my money on him.

I highly recommend Aaron's book, <u>The Athletic Advantage: 10 Lessons to Becoming A Premier Athlete.</u>

I recommend it because I have read it and I know the person who has lived it.

Keep moving forward.

Jim Glover

INTRODUCTION

When I was growing up all we did was jump rope, play basketball, or play tackle football in someone else's yard. You by no means played in your own yard, due to the fact that you didn't want your mom or dad to come outside if someone got hurt. I don't think it clicked with me that what we were actually doing was working out, just not with any type of weights. Working out to me was a thing of the past. Everyone liked to do it, but I didn't see the need to do it.

Our middle school in New Town, North Dakota, had a football team, but I'm not sure how serious I took it at that point. I was small, overweight, weak, and all I knew was if I didn't play some sport I was going to be in the band. There was no turning back. I didn't want to be in the band. So, I stuck it out and went for it. I got lit up in practice and also during the games, but there was no quit. I remember thinking during a game we played, "Why in the heck are we even out here today? It's cold as all get out and if I get hit it's going to hurt pretty bad." It was so cold and I knew that all I had to do was stick it out for four quarters and this game would be over. The game did end quicker than anticipated. I can't remember if we won. Once the horn sounded, I knew I just had to shake hands and go back to the school and change. It was OVER.

As I continued through sixth, seventh and eighth grade I didn't even think about what it meant to be an athlete. To be honest, I am not sure I even cared. I just wanted to go to practice, be on the team, and eat the snacks afterwards. Exercise, eating right, and getting into shape didn't even cross my mind.

Ninth grade came and went. I was only around 165 pounds at that time and I remember being at practice with all of these guys that were way bigger than I was, so instead of tackling them I stepped around them. I wasn't going to be the center of a huge laugh fest. I knew better than that. I would much rather get chewed out, than pick the grass and mud out of my facemask. One guy in particular on our team, Matthew Tant, was a Vanderbilt University commit back in 2000. I admired how huge this guy was and his work ethic on and off the field, but I was not about to get trucked by him in the middle of practice.

I believe it was a counter sweep play and I was playing defensive end. Down. Set. Hut. The QB handed the ball off to big ol' Matthew Tant. I looked up and said there is no way I'm tackling this dude. He's like three times the size of me. I'm puny and there ain't no way I'm bouncing off this guy like a pinball. Indeed, I didn't, I let him run on by me. Case was closed on that play.

I wouldn't call myself the most athletic, but during my tenth grade year I thought I might have something inside of me that would get me motivated to work out. That was a big negative as well. Just felt like a rolie polie. Big and round and ready to roll. I was more caught up in playing video games than trying to work out. I can't pinpoint which ones I was hooked on, but they were like a darn near leech that took all of my time, effort and energy. That's all I wanted to do. Video game after video game.

Then my best friend from school, Jacob, tried to encourage me to get rolling with some type of workout regimen. Unlike me, he had started working out with the beast of a running back I mentioned earlier. Jake was at some point curling 135 pounds on a straight bar, and that was impressive as a high school athlete. Jake looked like he could start for a college team as a high school sophomore. I knew he might be on to the secret sauce that I needed, but it wasn't until I met a guy named Wayne Collier that I decided to make an effort. And no, he is not my dad. Although my dad is Wayne as well.

Mr. Collier probably could have been my dad, but let's get to it. His son, Aaron, was an incoming freshman and I was pretty impressed with this kid. Here I was, 6'1" and maybe 195 pounds, and I had a fart in the wind's chance of being a starter. Aaron was a jacked freshman coming in and liked to workout. I had a brief conversation with Mr. Collier here and there, but never stuck to committing. It took a bit of convincing, but I took the plunge.

By the way, Mr. Collier was a former bodybuilder who competed in what I think was the early 1980s. I didn't like committing to working out, but I soon learned to like it. Some days it was tough, but I knew I had to suck it up and deal with it. If this dude had a son as a freshman who was yoked and looked like he ate nails for breakfast, I decided to listen. So, the journey started and there was no turning back.

You might be wondering why, of all people, would I listen to a bodybuilder for my workout advice? Well, I'm glad you asked.

1. Our high school Strength and Conditioning Program sucked. It was a whiteboard workout, a.k.a. find it online and write it on the white board. Heck that probably sounds like your coaches, too. Well, maybe they had the same workouts. Who knows, but I was always under the impression that when it was written on the board there was a race to see who could get it done the fastest.

2. Mr. Collier was in his late 40s or early 50s and this dude could rep out 225 pounds on squats more times than I've ever seen in my lifetime. Squats at the time equaled "not going to lift today" for me. Plus, I'd never seen any of my coaches demonstrate how to properly do a squat. So, I was definitely not listening to them. This dude practiced what he was

preaching to me. That was an EASY no brainer for me. LISTEN to this GUY!

3. He also had a structured workout plan. We tended to lift heavier sometimes, but then other times there were days that we went lighter for more reps. There was always some sort of cardio before or after the workout. Heck, I remember one time we even hopped into an ABS class at the gym. I was like, "I'm an offensive lineman, not some dude with a 6 pack." Let's just say I was hurting for quite a few days afterwards. It worked!!! I was finally going to see my ABS. Whelp, don't get excited because I've been searching for those bad boys for 33 years and counting and let's just say they are covered by a layer of love. Lots of love. Or baby fat? Your call!

So, in order to give you a brief run-down of what we did on a daily basis, I reached out to Wayne because what I thought was written down definitely was not in my notebook I used to keep track of. Keeping track always led to the best outcome. Here is a laid out, plain and simple 3-Week Rotation of what we did at the glorious Harpeth High School Fieldhouse and the infamous Boost Fit Club, before it got all corporate and stuff.

The Athletic Advantage

3-Week Rotation Training

Week 1

Monday: Chest and Back

Bench Press: x10, x8, x6, x4, x2, AMRAP* at least 15

(Increase weight as needed after each set)

One Arm Row: 3 x 10–16, each side

Incline Seated Chest Press: x8, x6, x4, x2

Single Arm Seated Chest Press: x8, x6, x4, x2

Standing Cable Chest Fly: 3 x 10–16

Lying Chest Fly: 3 x 10–16

*AMRAP = as many reps as possible

Tuesday: Leg Day

Back Squat: x10, x8, x6, x4 x2, AMRAP 135lbs

Leg Curls: 3 x 10–15

Leg Extensions: 3 x 10–15

Standing Calf Raises: 4 sets to failure

Seated Calf Raises: 3 sets to failure

Wednesday: REST Day or Cardio

Thursday: Shoulders and Arms

Seated Military Press: x10, x8, x6, x4, x2

Lateral Raises: 3 x 10–16

Straight Bar Upright Row: 3 x 10–16

Barbell Shrugs: 4 x 10–16

Straight Bar Biceps Curl: 3 x 10–16

Seated Hammer Curls: 3 x 10–16

Triceps Rope Extensions: 3 x 10–16

Single Arm Triceps Extensions: 3 x 10–16

Friday: Chest and Back

Bench Press: x12, x10, x8, x6

Pulldowns: 3 x 10–16

Incline Dumbbell Bench Press: x12, x10, x8, x6

Dumbbell Pullovers: 3 x 10–16

Bent Over T-Bar Rows: 3 x 10–16

Incline DB Chest Fly: 3 x 10–16

Weighted Cable Crunches: 3 x 25

WEEK 2

Monday: Legs

Back Squat: x10, x8, x6, x4 x2, AMRAP 145lbs

Leg Curls: 3 x 10–15

Leg Extensions: 3 x 10–15

Standing Calf Raises: 4 sets to failure

Seated Calf Raises: 3 sets to failure (Feet Wide, Feet Close)

Leg Press: 4 x 15–20 <u>or</u> Deadlifts: x10, x8, x6, x4, x2

Tuesday: Shoulders and Arms

Seated Military Press: x10, x8, x6, x4, x2

Lateral Raises: 3 x 10–16

Straight Bar Upright Row: 3 x 10–16

Barbell Shrugs: 4 x 10–16

Bicep Curls: 3 x 10–16

Seated Hammer Curls: 3x10–16

Triceps Rope Extensions: 3 x 10–16

Close Grip Bench Press: 3 x 10–15

Single Arm Tricep Extension: 3 x 10–16

Cable Rotations: 3 x 15

Wednesday: Rest Day

Thursday: Chest and Back

Bench Press: x12, x10, x8, x6

One Arm Row: 3 x 10–16

Incline Barbell Bench Press: x12, x10, x8, x6

Cable Straight Arm Pull Downs: 3 x 10–16

Bent Over Barbell Rows: 3 x 10–16

Dumbbell Chest Fly: 3 x 10–16

Weighted Sit Ups: 3 x 25

Friday: Heavy Legs

Leg Press: x15, x12, x10, x8, x6, AMRAP (aiming for 15–20 reps)

Barbell Split Lunge: 3 x 10

Single-Leg Leg Extensions: 3 x 10–16

Lying Leg Curls: 3 x 10–16

Standing Calf Raises: 3–5 x 15–20

Single-Leg Standing Calf Raises: 3 x 15, each leg

WEEK 3

Monday: Shoulders and Arms

Military Press: x12, x10, x8, x6, x4

Single Arm Lateral Raise: 3 x 10–16

Arnold Press: x10, x8, x6, x4

Dumbbell Shrugs: 3 x 10–15 (Hold at the top for 2 count.)

Dumbbell Hammer Curls: 3 x 10–16

Preacher Curls: 3 x 10–16

Biceps 21's: 3 x 21

10 LESSONS TO BECOMING A PREMIER ATHLETE

Dumbbell Close Grip Bench Press: 3 x 10–16

Seated Overhead Triceps Extension: 3 x 10–16

Standing Triceps Extension: 3–4 x 10–20

Tuesday: Chest and Back

Decline Bench Press: x12, x10, x8, x6

Bench Press: x12, x10, x8, x6, AMRAP 135lbs or 185lbs

Wide Grip Pulldowns: 3 x 10–16

Bent Over Rear Dumbbell Fly: 3 x 10–16

Seated Cable Pullover: 3 x 10–16

Cable Fly: 3 x 10–16, 1 x AMRAP

Wednesday: Rest Day

Thursday: Leg Day

Back Squat: x10, x8, x6, x4, x2, AMRAP 145lbs

Deadlifts: x10, x8, x6, x4, x2

Leg Curls: 4 x 10–20

Leg Extensions: 4 x 10–20

Lunges: 3 x 10

Standing Calf Raises: 4 sets to failure

Seated Calf Raises: 3 sets to failure (Feet Wide, Feet Close)

Friday: Heavy Shoulders and Arms

Military Press: x12, x10, x8, x6, x4

Single Arm Lateral Raise: 3 x 10–16

Arnold Press: x10, x8, x6, x4

Barbell Shrugs: 3 x 15–20

Dumbbell Hammer Curls: 3 x 10–16

Preacher Curls: 3 x 10–16

Biceps 21's: 3 x 21

Dumbbell Close Grip Bench Press: 3 x 10–16

Seated Overhead Triceps Extensions: 3 x 10–16

Standing Triceps Extensions: 3–4 x 10–20

10 LESSONS TO BECOMING A PREMIER ATHLETE

It might seem redundant or maybe even boring to some, but we always had ways to make the workout fun no matter how much was being lifted.

Wayne also had a bet with me, but I could never seem to grasp it. He tended to mess with me about not being able to do pull-ups. I was able to do 1–2 all of the time, but I could never get past the hump. He said, "If you can ever get those 10 pull-ups in a row I'll stop bugging you or giving you a hard time about not being able to do the reps." Well, who would have guessed that almost 15 years later, I still can't do 10 full bodyweight pull-ups to perfection. So, he still has bragging rights in that regard.

Some days during these workouts things went well, but other days were a struggle. I think the best part about the workouts themselves was that I was being challenged and held accountable for getting the job done. Like I mentioned earlier, the school workouts were a bit bogus and it just seemed like it was a race to the finish line for most. I didn't want to rush it, and I also didn't really believe that the workouts at school were worth a crap. Let's be honest, our coach wasn't in the best of shape. It was tough for me to follow through with someone who didn't even work out themselves.

You could even say that I tended to enjoy leg day more than most. It was something about getting the weight up on the last set. The rep set was supposed to be tough, but each and every week that went by the rep set weight started to creep up. That only meant one thing to me, PROGRESS. I was getting stronger. I started out with 135 pounds for the rep set and by the end of my senior year I was repping 225 pounds for at least 15–20 reps. It felt like I was going to puke most of those days, but I think it made me a better person. Taught me not to give up and to never settle for just doing the lightest weight. I wanted to be pushed. So, I pushed myself to the limit on quite a few of those days. Reps until failure and it felt as if you might even pass out a bit after these sets.

Mr. Collier helped me with finding satisfaction and pleasure in pushing myself. Eventually he helped me with my next struggle... to put on more physical mass. I had struggled all through high school to gain weight and it just wasn't happening. My parents kept buying more and more food, and I kept eating it, but I just couldn't budge the number on the scale to increase to the upper 190s. My freshman year of school I think I was around 170 pounds and could basically wear my friend Daniel's clothes. A size 30–32 shorts/jeans and a large shirt. Well, let's be honest, I was really small and had no chance of thinking about playing sports at the next level at this weight. I was undersized and tried everything I could think of to try and put on weight.

Mr. Collier gave me some ideas around how I could gain more weight. I ended up trying hard boiled eggs for breakfast, adding in a couple of protein shakes to the mix as well, and heck I ended up eating quite a few double cheese burgers as well. Tuna fish sandwiches were also in the mix. I'm not a huge fan, so I didn't stick with those for very long. My protein shakes consisted of a protein/weight gainer from a website we used to use called nutritionexpress.com.

The name escapes me on which protein/weight gainer we used, but I know it was a 5-pound container and the recommended serving was four scoops per shake. Well, I'm one of those who tried the 4 scoops and decided that I was going to go through this tub of protein real fast at that rate. So, I dropped it to 2 scoops and added in 2–4 raw eggs, 2% milk (usually about 16–24 ounces), 1–2 scoops of peanut butter and sometimes even chocolate syrup. Not healthy by any means now that I am looking back at it, but I was trying new and different things to help with the boost in weight gain. I felt as if my parents were going to make me get a job during the school year just to help pay for groceries. Luckily, I didn't have to do such a thing. Let's just say that I caught on to how this whole weight gaining was supposed to happen and from the end of my junior year of high school, which is when I started to workout, until my senior season, I went from somewhere around 190 pounds to 210 pounds. Thanks, Mr. Collier! Twenty pounds was a big jump, but I was still a bit undersized. Too slow for linebacker or defensive end. Just a solid offensive lineman at best.

Towards the end of the senior season I started to get some looks from college. I ended the season with the All Region Offensive Lineman Award and Academic All Region Award, so I suppose that stuck out for coaches. There was only one school that had my attention since they were the only school to offer me a scholarship to play. It was a small school in Jackon, TN, called Lambuth University. I had never heard of it before, but I went on a visit and decided that it was my best option. I earned a partial football scholarship and mostly academic scholarship to get me through my first year.

Before I headed off to Lambuth I had to be sure that I was in the best shape of my life. I didn't know what to expect as far as a conditioning test or run test. All I was worried about was the expectations I had set for myself. I was going to pass it no matter how tough or easy it was. So, like I did before my senior year of school, I went to work out with Mr. Collier.

We had grueling workouts after I had already worked eight hours of hard labor at Hillwood Country Club during the day. I spent days of the hot sun beating down on me in the summer and then another 1–2 hours in the gym just to play college ball. It never really seemed worth it, or that's what other people were thinking. Nobody could ever wrap their head around it. They weren't in my shoes, so they didn't know what I had in mind when I told them I was going to play college football. They always wanted me to do other things after work and I quickly told them NO. I had to prioritize my workouts. These folks hated that answer, because quite frankly they were not going to college for sports. I had to have a different mindset and not let anything get in my way. Heck during this time I might have made some folks mad or even lost a few friends because of it, but thinking back they were more of a distraction anyways.

During the time I was training I struggled with my conditioning, being an asthmatic. I could never get things under control with my breathing. I was always relying on my inhaler and I couldn't get over the hump. I wasn't motivated to run. I hated it. So, Cal Sullivan offered to help me with this. He was a soccer player in high school, but the cool thing was he was going to Lambuth for soccer. This was a breeze for him. He knew he didn't have to help me, but he went out of his way to encourage me and push me until the breaking point.

We would start out with one lap around the track at the school, then we would make a sharp turn out the chain link fence that covered the football field. Trekking down the street then a hard right down into the Woodlands neighborhood. By the time we made that hard right turn I was about to turn around and walk back, but Cal wasn't going to let that happen. He was already a good way ahead of me, but he was yelling positive feedback along the way. The struggle was real, but I was determined to finish. Along the street going into the Woodlands neighborhood it started out flat and then it gradually became an incline. That was the worst part. Coming ahead was a 3-way stop. At the stop sign we took another right and went to the cul-de-sac and came back for the same stop sign. It kept going. Another hard right and we were in the clear for a bit with hills. Upon us was another right turn. We headed down another long road that never seemed to end.

Sometimes while running, my best friend's dad would be outside and he would give me a look and say, "Why the heck are you running? It's way too hot out here for that." My response, "Conditioning for Football." I was on my way. I could barely utter those words, by the way. I'm pretty sure at some point Cal thought I was either lost or I died along the trail. Yet he never gave up on me no matter how slow I was. The final stretch of this run seemed like 5 miles. It stretched from one part of the Woodlands neighborhood all the way to the Fieldhouse. At some point and time, I turned on my inner Forrest Gump and just kicked it into another gear. You never think you have the last little bit of energy to push through, but time and time again I did it. I conquered the running even though I sucked at it. I checked it off the list time and time again.

Even though I sacrificed a ton of things to get to where I was going, I'm not sure I have any regrets about it. I was self-motivated to be the best and that's what I was destined to do. Most run with rap music in the headphones, but not this guy. ROCKY 4 soundtrack on repeat. If I was feeling it on a song, I just kept it on repeat until I got tired of it. So, thanks to Cal Sullivan and the Rocky 4 soundtrack I accomplished a lot over the Summer.

Summer was winding down, so it was time to report to football camp at Lambuth University. I can't pinpoint what day I went to Jackson, TN, but I know it was early July. Upon arrival, we parked and started making our way for football check-ins. It took quite a while because all of the players were reporting at one time. We stood in line meeting other guys and cutting up until it was our turn. Once I gave my name and was cleared, I received my laundry pin for football clothes, as well as two pairs of shorts and two Lambuth Shirts. These were our practice/workout clothes. Walking past the chapel on campus led me down the long sidewalk to the gymnasium area where the football locker rooms were located. It was small and like any other locker room it didn't have the most pleasant of smells, but what the heck. I claimed my spot and off I went to unload all of my belongings into the dorm room.

My dorm room was located on the 4th floor of Sprague Hall. It was a small campus, so trying to find the dorm room wasn't very hard at all. Now we were off hauling things up four flights of stairs because there was no elevator. I met my roommate upon moving in. He was from Ohio. He was a bit taller than I was, but that really didn't matter. I'm pretty sure it took all day to get things settled like I wanted them, plus all of the trips back and forth to Wal-Mart. I had Hulk Hogan posters on the wall, my stereo over by my tv, and my clothes all tucked away in the tiny closet.

Saturday had come and gone. Sunday was the day that all of the football players were going to go to chapel as a team. That we did. We walked as a team down to the Methodist Church about four blocks from campus. Well, everyone except the guys who already got homesick, including my roommate I was telling you about. One day in and he was already packing the things he had unpacked the night before to head back to Ohio. I didn't understand why guys would travel all of this way and then want to bail after one day. But, he did.

Chapel went well. It was a bit different, but I managed to get through the service in one piece. After service, I do believe we had to be at the local doctor's office that afternoon for our sports physicals. That was an interesting event. All football players at one time at one clinic. Waiting was the hard part. As I sat, I was approached by two upper class offensive lineman who were there to get their physical as well, but they had one interesting question they wanted to ask me, "Are you Aymish or Amish?" I was confused by the question, but I guess when I stood 6'1" and had a shaved head, no mustache, and a full beard, they might be confused as well. I stated I was neither, but they insisted on telling me that I was, so it turns out that after only about 48 hours of being on campus I had a new nickname, "Jebediah." This wasn't a name a few people called me, it was everybody. My friends, their parents, coaches, staff, and so on. It's been 15 years since I stepped foot on Lambuth's campus and I still get called "Jebediah" til this day. You could consider this a name that has lasted a lifetime.

Next on the list was the conditioning test and the lifting test, which happened on Monday. I was excited for the lifting test mainly because I knew I was stronger than ever before, so I was fired up about it. The other part was the run test. I dreaded this more than anything else. Our lifting test consisted of how many reps we could bench press 225 pounds, big skill players had to lift 205 pounds, and skill players 185 pounds. We already had a goal that was set by our coaches because we were offensive lineman. 15 reps was the magic number. I started with a few warm up sets, just to be sure I was ready to go. Nothing worse than thinking you are warmed and ready for lifting then you pull a muscle. Not a good sign.

135 pounds was what I picked for about 10–15 warm up reps to be sure I was nice and loose. I then increased it to 185 pounds for about 8–10 reps. I was all set to get things rolling. 225 pounds was loaded on the bar and a huge wave of fear set in. What if I didn't get these reps? I'd worked hard all summer to get to this point and I didn't want to let myself down. The bar came unloaded off of the safety hooks and that

first rep went down and up easily. I couldn't believe how easy the first 10 reps actually were. Smooth like butter! 10 turned into 15. It was getting a bit tougher, but I knew that I couldn't stop at 15. 15 was the minimum. I kept pushing for a few more even though my chest was burning from the work being put in. I capped out at 19 reps before I had to rack it back up.

Coach Emmons was fired up, but stated, "Why did you stop?" I said I got what I needed to, so I thought I was done. He didn't like that answer, but that was 50% completion on what had to be done for the day.

Looking ahead to the run test was brutal. I had no idea what to expect. Was it ten 100-yard dash sprints for time or was it the mile run test? Since I had already passed the lifting test, all I had to do was pass the run test and I was in the clear for any type of punishment that was headed my way. The goal for the run test was to make it five times around the perimeter of the field in your allotted time frame. If I am not mistaken, the linemen had to be around the field in about 90 seconds. The big guys were up and everyone took off. Lots of huffing and puffing from a lot of guys, which didn't make it look very promising for me. I was 6'1", 235 pounds and an asthmatic. Although the first lap was the real test, I made it in the time frame given. The goal wasn't to sprint full speed for all five, but to pace yourself. Once you made it to the finish line you had enough recovery until the skill guys got finished. I ended up finishing the second, third, and fourth lap around the field. When it was all said and done I had set out and accomplished exactly what I had to do. Five laps in the time frame that was given by the coaches. Linemen had 90 seconds, big skill players had 70 seconds, and skill players had 60 seconds.

I might as well brag and let you know that I was the only lineman who made my lift test and run test, so I didn't have to get up at 5 a.m. and do any workouts with Coach Hillie. He was the guy who you didn't want to make mad. Former military officer who liked to make your life miserable if you missed your times, meetings, or workouts. I was excited that I didn't have to get up in the mornings like a lot of my friends did, at 5 a.m. or O'Dark Thirty.

I learned a lot of things before, during, and after college. Some of those lessons learned led me to where I am today. I started out as a college athlete, but felt as though there was nothing in it for me after 2 years. I had given everything I had, but the coaching staff felt otherwise. After an injury, it was time to move on from athlete to college student. I ended up at UT Martin to finish up my undergraduate degree. It took me another year to complete since some of my credits didn't transfer.

Once I graduated, I set myself up for success with the 2009 job market. Anyone who remembers 2009, it was the downfall of the economy and that made it hard to find a job that I wanted. I tried and tried, but ended up with something way outside of my expertise. I started out my post college career working in a grocery store. It was a job, but obviously not the one I had hoped for.

I learned a lot about the grocery business and what it took to run a successful store with multiple employees. I learned how to create purchase orders, run the registers, and manage some of the departments to keep products on the shelves while managing exactly the products people were likely to purchase.

I had been at the grocery store for about two years before I decided to make the jump to apply to graduate school and further my education. I ended up applying to 3 schools, but only completed one of those applications. The only one I finished was exactly where I wanted to be. Florida State University had a new graduate student and I was headed there to start the school year off January 2010. I zipped through my time there, so I could get a real job this time.

Before I graduated I spent 3 months of my internship at Mayo Clinic where I worked with the Cardiac and Pulmonary Rehabilitation Team. My focus was working with patients who were on the transplant list or who had already had a transplant to get back in shape to be discharged in a timely manner. We worked on strength training, flexibility, and cardiovascular exercise each day. I had a great time working with the team at Mayo Clinic partly because I was challenged in many ways. Not only was I challenged while in the clinic working with a ton of different patients, but I got to spend time with some of the top doctors in the world, observing their surgical practices. I observed a cardiac ablation, stent procedure and an atrial fibrillation procedure. All of these were intriguing to say the least, because I had no idea how any of these procedures were conducted until those days. I came away with a ton more knowledge than before after all these surgeries.

After I completed my internship, it was time to graduate from Florida State University with my Masters degree in Exercise Physiology. It was time to conquer the world a second time. I had all of the tools necessary to begin the new job hunt post graduation—or so I thought. I applied and applied to a ton of jobs in the market as I had just moved back to Nashville since graduating. With not a whole lot of luck in sight since I didn't have much experience, I went back to work with my father-in-law at his grocery store.

All of this was all too familiar as I was working here right before I had left for graduate school. Nothing had really changed except for a bit of the layout of the store, so it wasn't too big of a learning curve.

During the time I was at the store, I got my Personal Training Certification via American College of Sports Medicine. I took it twice as the first time I missed the passing score by 1 point. Then I was official and I went looking for a few more job opportunities.

The first call for an interview I received was from the downtown YMCA in Nashville. Laura gave me a shot to become a member of the YMCA and to be a front desk associate. I nailed the interview and got the confirmation call a few days later to solidify my new job at the Y. I continued working at the store during this time, but I had to adjust my hours of work since I had to be at the Y early in the morning.

I continued to work both jobs until I came across a full-time position with a company called Healthways. Healthways worked with fortune 500 companies to help employee health satisfaction. If employees of these companies were triggered for the health coaching programs, they had to participate in order to get a reduced health care cost. I interviewed and got this job as well. So, I let my father-in-law know that it was time to pass the torch and move on to the real world. He was fine with that as he already knew my time was limited with him at the store until I found something that I was really interested in.

For my new schedule, I went to work at the YMCA from 4:45 a.m. to 10 .a.m. then I went on to Healthways from 1 p.m. to 9 p.m. I got the best of both worlds, as I was selling memberships in the morning and working on health behavior change in the evening. I gained experience and became a well rounded individual within the health and fitness world.

I spent a ton of time going back and forth between these two jobs for the next few years, but I did manage to squeeze in a bit more workload by taking on a volunteer position at the Vanderbilt Dayani Center in their Cardiac and Pulmonary department. I was determined to volunteer my way to the top, but it was more of a hands off approach instead of hands on. It was a little bit tougher to land a job there, but the experience was well worth it.

Over the course of the next few years working all three of the positions, I learned a lot about what I actually wanted to do with my career. I had sold memberships, started to do some personal training, run bootcamps, health coaching, and volunteering. It was a lot for one person to handle, but I tried to fit it all in.

I was starting to get a bit burned out with the YMCA and Healthways as I had with some previous jobs. I want to be challenged in the workplace and some of the tasks at hand were redundant and getting a bit old.

So, I reached out to a friend of mine who was doing some training at an orthopedic clinic. He put in a good word and within a few weeks I had my interview for what I thought was my dream job. It seemed as if it was going to be. All of the right things were said in the interview, the pay was a bit more than what I was currently getting, and it seemed as if I would have a bit more flexibility with my schedule.

After I received the call about getting the job at the orthopedic clinic, I gave Healthways my 2-week notice. On the one hand I was sad to go, but I was also ready to try something new for a change.

I went in not knowing anything about how to train someone with orthopedic issues or if I would even have a client when I started. I was going into this to build my book of clients as I didn't have anyone. Or so I thought! Then, just a day before I started, another trainer turned in her notice. I expected to walk in and start from scratch. Instead I walked into a full schedule on Day 1.

THE ATHLETIC ADVANTAGE

I got to train semi-professional athletes, professional athletes, entrepreneurs, large business owners and just all around cool people who wanted to get in shape. Things were really shaping up for me. The clients loved me and I had one of the highest retention rates as a trainer this place had ever seen. My buddy Elliott had the highest retention rate as he had been there a bit longer than I had. That was to be expected. I was getting asked by management to train some VIP members, which was at the time winning in my book.

Everyone wanted me to train them, but it was starting to take a toll. I was getting to the gym at 5 a.m., six days a week, to train 40–50 hours per week. I was getting no sleep, my eating habits were way off track and I had started to creep up on my weight over the past 12 months. I was working like a dog and it was taking a toll on my health. I was snoring a ton more, I was heavier than when I played college sports, and my bagel intake was at an all time high.

Things just were not what I thought this job was going to be. I started to speak up and give my opinion on things and it didn't come across as that. Management took it as complaining, so within the next 6 months I was FIRED! Yep, canned on a Wednesday a week after my birthday. This hadn't even crossed my mind. I was speaking up and giving my thoughts on things that I thought should happen and the next thing you know I was out of a job.

I was angry, frustrated, and caught off guard, but this was just what I needed to fuel my next journey in my career. For the next several months I went to work for Six 1 Five sports training in Mt. Juliet, TN. I was teaching bootcamp classes and training sports performance groups as well. When I wasn't teaching I was taking the bootcamp class myself. It was time to regain my health and take control of my life.

I taught classes and took classes from January to August of 2013. This is where the change happened. I lost 50 pounds during that time and regained my energy, eating habits, and sleep pattern to set forth on the journey of entrepreneurship. I was still working for Six 1 Five, but knew I wanted to do my own thing eventually. Like starting my own business.

All of the jobs I had previously led me to the road of being an entrepreneur. I learned a lot from these past experiences, but now it was time to take life by the horns and be a business owner. This is where Premier Performance Training LLC in Franklin, TN, comes in. I left Six 1 Five Sports training after I had built up an established clientele in Williamson County. From there I built a well established business working with Adults and Sports Performance Training called Premier Performance Training LLC.

Now I want to share 10 lessons I learned that helped me get to the place I am today. In the next few chapters I'll break down these lessons and give you my top three tips, as well as a client story that connects to the lesson. Not all lessons and stories are the same, so stay tuned!

CHAPTER 1

DISCIPLINE, verb:
to train oneself to
do something in a
controlled and
habitual way

I used discipline as the driving force to keep me on track with the things I wanted to accomplish. It took a lot of time, effort, and energy to get to the day of the running and lifting test, but without self-discipline I would not have gotten there. I shut off a ton of people to focus on the things that I wanted to do, which paid off. I pretty much had the same routine before I got to college. Get Up, Eat Breakfast, Go to Work, Workout, Go Home, Eat, Go to Sleep. Once I got one of these things screwed up or out of order, it threw everything else off. Whereas the more I stuck to this routine, the more habitual it became, and it made it easier and easier to get up and look forward to the day. Tons of distractions came and went, but at the end of the day I had a goal to accomplish.

As things began to settle down a bit and I got to meet a few more of my teammates and even hang out with them a bit, I began to develop some friendships with a few of the guys. Now I had no idea what high school they came from or even how good they were. All I knew was that they had the same opportunity that I had, and it was to play football.

Morgan Cruce. He was from Obion County and he came to Lambuth as a slot receiver/fullback.

Grant Horton. He was from Williamson County and Played at Centennial High School. He came to Lambuth as a defensive back.

10 LESSONS TO BECOMING A PREMIER ATHLETE

Brent Pierce. Hometown guy from Jackson. Went to Jackson Southside and came to Lambuth as a linebacker.

I wouldn't say I was any better than any of these guys because we all played different positions. I was with the big sloppy dudes and they spent time with those who actually had some sort of speed. What I do know is that we got along with each other for the most part. We went to Peking Chinese Buffet all the time.

I almost killed Brent one afternoon, though. Morgan and I were talking and Brent took a drink of Sweet Tea and about that time I said a not so nice joke. All I remember next was some obnoxious coughing and wheezing while Brent was trying to come up for his next breath of air.

We went to the movies together, we spent time at each other's houses, well mainly Brent and Morgan's since they lived so close to campus. We played Halo on the original Xbox for countless hours throughout the day and even after study hall on most evenings. I'm still not sure how we all ended up with a 4.0 GPA during our first semester. Between early football workouts, practice, class, study hall, chapel, and film work, we still managed to get our work done.

I fell asleep before the other guys did on a consistent basis, so they found it funny to turn off the music I had on or to mess with me while I slept. I could have been dead asleep, but I knew when someone messed with my radio. I was ready to fight someone once it got turned off. I hopped up quicker than the Undertaker did. On other occasions, they would run by the hallway door, since ours was open 90% of the time since Grant went to sleep around 1 a.m., and throw things and try to hit me in the face. Sometimes it was Skittles, other times I have no idea, but I do remember hanging Morgan over the stair railing ready to push him over. They had run by numerous times and hit me in the forehead, so I had had enough. I was ready to make things right, but he wasn't ready for what I had in store. A quick apology was rendered even though I think Brent was the culprit.

Discipline was needed to keep myself and my teammates on track to what we were going to accomplish. Whether that was the workouts we were finishing or the school work that needed to be completed as well. Discipline was key.

Here are three things that helped me stay disciplined during this time:

1. **Keep a detailed schedule.** Writing down the things you need to accomplish will take you places. Whether I was scheduling workouts or tutoring, writing it down led me to stay on track.

2. **Stick to what works.** Don't change things unless they are not working. Stay the course and don't worry about what happens next.

3. **Accountability.** In order to stay disciplined with the task at hand it was always best to have someone hold me accountable. Whether that was a teammate or roommate it didnt matter.

Meet Mike Archie

He's a former NFL running back who stuck to a very strict regimen to keep him in shape. He worked out just as much if not more than the next guy who was trying to make it pro. I met Mike at my former place of employment. He was a 5-Star Running Back in Pennsylvania in high school and was so good he got drafted by the Tennessee Oilers (Titans). Mike was not your average athlete growing up. He held the scoring record at his local high school, as well as the rushing record. He was a great two-sport athlete and dominated when he played. With all of the sports he played he was in great shape and never seemed to be injured. It wasn't until he was done playing in the NFL that had him sidelined for months on in. Mike was playing basketball with his kids in the backyard when he went in for a crossover layup and all of a sudden his ankle gave out. He had ruptured his achilles tendon.

That's where we met and we hit it off like best friends. He had completed his 6–9 month physical therapy stent and was looking for someone to help him shed those unwanted pounds he had gained during the process and get back in shape. Mike was determined to do whatever it took to get to a point where he was back in playing shape. He had been through a torn achilles, gained weight, had increased blood pressure, and was not feeling well at all. We started with an initial evaluation to determine what it was he wanted to accomplish. His number one goal was to get back into the best shape he had ever been in. That was the shape he was in in college. I had my work cut out for me, but I agreed to take this challenge on and I wasn't going to back down. Being Disciplined was easy due to Mike being a former athlete. He committed to training three times a week and started to watch what he was eating day in and day out as well. That is the key. Stay on track, schedule the workouts, and results will follow.

We took a 3-day split to focus on. Day 1, Chest/Back and Cardio. Day 2, Lower Body. And Day 3, Shoulders and Arms. It was a bit brutal on most days, but he stuck with it. Coming back from an injury is difficult, so you have to be determined and disciplined to be the best once you set your mind up for success. Mike did this and ended up dropping over 30 pounds, reduced his blood pressure medicine, and he even was getting some compliments asking if he still played in the NFL. You know he felt awesome about this because he hadn't played in years.

Scheduling his workouts, sticking to the plan that was working, and having me and his family for accountability was the perfect workout pill for Mike to swallow. That setback that Mike faced was years ago and with that discipline he instilled into his mindset and regimen, he still trains to this day. Nothing is stopping him from being in the best shape possible before he turns 50. We have just under two years to get him there.

Be like Mike and stay disciplined with your goals.

CHAPTER 2

FRIENDSHIP, noun:
the emotions or
conduct of friends:
the state of being
friends

So many lasting friendships were born as freshman at
Lambuth University. We didn't even know each other
before then—I think that's the cool part about this
whole story. Yet we attended weddings except for
Grant, our kids' birthday parties, except for Grant,
and we tried every time we could to spend time with

one another if we happened to be in the same city at the same time. Heck, after I transferred schools, I still went over to Morgan's parents' home even when he wasn't there. It was about a 20-minute drive when I was at University of Tennessee at Martin. Best 20-minute drive ever. These are the kind of friendships that I would have never found if I had never committed to go to Lambuth University.

We went on overnight camping trips with some of the other guys in the dorm as well. Heck, one weekend we got so bored we slicked down the hallway for a slip and slide. It started off great, but ended horribly wrong. Stephen, one of the guys who lived next door to us, decided it was his turn to take off and slide as far as he could down the hallway. He backed up as far as he could and he was off. Sliding like a greased pig down a slide. He had great speed and it took a ton of effort to get the distance he was aiming for, but as soon as he was embarking on the completion of his hallway journey he popped up real quick. He popped us real quick and descended just as fast. He had hopped up super quick and sliced a huge gash in his back on the metal portion of the fire alarm. The alarm never went off, but Stephen was done and so were we. We attempted the lame male First Aid with bandages and ointment and sent him on his way the rest of the day. Our sliding days were over. Stephen made a full recovery, but I will never forget the janitors asking us for probably a week straight, "Why are the floors so slick?" I played it off like nothing ever happened.

These types of things probably should have had us kicked out, but we got away with it.

As we continued to try and stay out of trouble doing mischievous things, we still had to go to workouts and our practice because at the end of the day we were still a part of the football team. In high school, through every practice and game played I had never had an injury. Whether that was an ankle, knee, hip, or shoulder, it never happened. It wasn't until my freshman year at Lambuth that I had what I thought was a career ending injury. The offensive lineman was working on some pass blocking drills when my name was called and was up. Down, Set, Hut was called and as I was going back to set my feet, my right knee buckled. I wasn't sure what happened, but I knew it didn't feel normal. There was quite a bit of pain and discomfort. I tried to shake it off, but the pain just wasn't going away. I was done at practice, so I went to see the athletic trainer. The athletic trainer, Jason, took a look at what was going on. He didn't know what to think of it since it was kind of a fluke thing that happened, but he ended up doing some strengthening tests on it. I disliked everything he tried to do because it made the pain worse. Bad enough that I could barely walk back to the dorm. I was making the walk back to Sprague Hall limping and there were no elevators. It hurt to walk up the stairs due to the throbbing pain that I was experiencing.

I continued to go to the athletic trainer for days on end with very little progress. Leg lifts, quad strengthening exercises, stem, and ice. Rinse and repeat for a week or so. Things were still not getting better, so I opted to drive to Martin, TN, and see an orthopedic doctor from Vanderbilt. It took forever to get in to see this guy, but it was totally worth it. My dad had seen him years ago for his knee surgeries, so I know we had a good one on our hands. Once again, he did some testing and he determined that I had some bad quadriceps to hamstring strength ratio and it was causing the severe pain and discomfort in my knee. That slight kick back on the pass blocking drill caused it all and I was out for the remainder of my freshman year of football. Even though I wasn't a starter, I did hate that I had to sit out and observe from the sidelines. For the next few months my days consisted of standing on the sidelines at practice, going to the athletic trainer, working out my upper body, and trying to strengthen my lower body by using very light weights and taking advantage of the swimming pool. This was a tough spot to be since I had never been injured before. I didn't really know how to take it. It was frustrating at times and at other times I wanted to just be done with football. While on the injured list, these friendships held true. My friends helped me get to and fro, as well as, waited on me to walk to class even though it was a struggle. Here are the top three ways I find building lifelong friendships happen:

1. **Common Interests.** All my friends played the same sport I did so this made it extremely easy to stay connected. They also like playing video games a bit, so that helped as well. Working out was another interest we shared as well. If you are going to be playing sports and not working out, then there will be plenty

of struggle for you. Just by having these few things in common it definitely helped.

2. **Family Values.** Having your family around to support each and every move was a huge positive. We would even go to each other's houses to hang out on the weekends. Well, mainly Morgan's and Brent's. They took us in just like we were family. Fed us, helped out if needed, and always invited us over no matter what the situation was.

3. **Staying Grounded.** We all have friends who think they are invincible and no matter what you tell them, they do the opposite. Having friends who would keep me grounded was a plus. They would call me out if they thought a decision was not in my best interest or would question things if they knew it wasn't going to be helpful. This helped in the long run even though I probably didn't see that initially. These friends wouldn't let my ego get bigger than it was actually supposed to.

10 LESSONS TO BECOMING A PREMIER ATHLETE

Working out in a gym might be the last place you might think about making lifelong friendships, but you can't count it out. Most folks have differing personalities and might not like working out with other people.

I get that, but I've also seen the opposite. I have seen people with different political views, religious views, etc., become great friends over the years. It's about more than getting a great workout.

Here at Premier Performance Training we have built a sense of community that no matter what your opinion is on things, we can still come together for the ultimate goal of getting better one day at a time and living a healthier lifestyle. I enjoy introducing new members to our super star clients who have been with us for years.

One: it helps break the ice and release a bit of that stress and fear that people have when they walk through our doors. Two: it creates an initial relationship with people who have different stories of their own they can share and connect with. Three: it creates business or sometimes business deals within our community once people understand who each other are and what they do for a living. This might be the best thing we have going here at Premier Performance Training. Lifelong friendships and relationships with others in the community.

Meet Justin Smitherman and Benjamin Drumwright

Justin and Benjamin came to work out with me one day after their moms' decided it was a good idea for both of them to workout together.

Benjamin was enrolled at Brentwood High and he played football and threw shot put for track. Justin was the starting running back for Ravenwood High School. They were both pumped to be in and get rocking with the workout. I turned around to get things rolling when both of the guys had this super awkward look on their faces. I was like, "What's going on? You both know each other, right?"

Ben and Justin both looked at me and said, "No, our moms know each other, but this is the first time we have met."

I was surprised, but I guess moms know what's best, because Justin and Benjamin continued to work out with each other 2 to 3 times a week for about 6 months. During that time they both improved their strength and endurance, and increased their body weight. They also bonded over mutual suffering and hard work, and became good friends even though they went to rival schools.

I have a feeling their friendship is a friendship that will last—just like so many other lifelong friendships that began on Day One at the Premier Performance Training facility. We want this to not only be a place to get healthy, but also a place where you can meet lifelong friends as well. Build Community and Become Friends for a Lifetime.

CHAPTER 3

> *PERSEVERANCE,*
> *noun: persistence*
> *in doing something*
> *despite difficulty or*
> *delay in achieving*
> *success*

Even though I had never been injured before, I had to make the best of it. I supported my teammates during practice and on the field during game days even though I didn't really want to be there. I went to the training room and talked with other teammates who were on the injured list as well. It was great to connect and find ways to make others feel better because we were all in the same boat—injured and unable to do anything.

There were two ways to look at this situation: quit and move on or make the most of this and get healthy and back on the field. I chose the latter. It took a lot of hard work and determination to do so, but I did. I spent numerous hours at the athletic training office and in the weight room to try and get healthy. It took a lot of perseverance to overcome my injury, but by the time spring ball came around I was stronger and better than ever. I was persistent in the rehab process and I was persistent with the weight training because I knew that my playing time was not over. As I take a look back it was an amazing feat for me to overcome.

As things started to progress, my confidence started to increase. I was able to do more and more in the weight room and on the field. It took a while to get comfortable with a bunch of the lifts we had to perform, but I had better get to learning them. Once I was cleared to go back to working out with the team, the workout tended to look a bit as follows. Here are a couple of sample weeks of what we had to go through.

WEEK 3

Monday

Power Clean: 4x50%, 4x55%, 3x60%, 3x2x70%

Bench Press: 3x6 (medium weight) 1x5 (medium weight)

Incline Bench Press: 1x12 (heavy weight), 1x10 (heavy weight)

Lat Circuit: 3x10

DB Bench Press: 3x8

Standing Military Press: 3x10

36's x2

Arm Blast (10 minutes of Biceps, Triceps, Shoulders)

Abs

Tuesday

Back Squat: warm up, 1x20, 1x15, 1x12, 1x10, 1x8 (medium weight)

Front Squat: 3x8 (medium weight)

Step Front Lunge: 3x4x3 (135lbs and above)

Clean Shrugs: 4x4x90% of clean max

Body Weight Leg Curls: x2

Leg Curls: 3x10

Leg Extensions: 3x10

Abs

Wednesday

Active Rest

Warm-Up

Stretch

1 Mile Run

Thursday

Incline Bench Press: Warm Up, 2x6, 2x5 (medium weight)

Bench Press (for volume): 1x12, 1x10 (heavy weight)

Dumbbell Incline Press: 3x10

High Pulls: 3x10

Bent Over Rows: 3x10

Close Grip Bench Press: 3x10

Lat Pulldown: 3x12

Arm Blast (10 minutes of Biceps, Triceps, Shoulders)

Abs

Friday

Hang Clean with Squat: 3x6x65% (Clean Max)

Single Leg Squat: 2x12

Romanian Deadlift: 3x10

Hyperextension: 2x20 (25–45lbs Plate)

Single Leg Extension: 2x10

Manual Leg Curl: 3x8

Abs

Week 4

Monday

Power Clean: 1 Rep Max

Bench Press: 3–5 Rep Max

Back Squats: 3–5 Rep Max

Lat Circuit: 3x10

Arm Blast (10 minutes of Biceps, Triceps, Shoulders)

Abs

Wednesday

Power Clean: 5x65%, 3x70%, 3x80%, 3x85%, 1x90%, 2x85%

Squats: 8x50%, 5x60%, 5x70%, 5x75%, 5x85%, 5x80%

Clean Shrugs: 4x4x85%

Step Front Lunge: 3x4x3

Leg Curls: 3x10

Leg Extensions: 3x10

Body Weight Leg Curls: x2

Romanian Deadlift: 3x10

Hyperextension: 2x20

Abs

Friday

Bench Press: 5x50%, 5x75%, 3x85%, 2x90%, 2x1x95%, 185-225lbs Burnout

Incline Bench Press: 4x8

Lat Pulldowns: 3x12

1 Arm Dumbbell Rows: 3x10

Close Grip Bench Press: 3x10

Arm Blast (10 minutes of Biceps, Triceps, Shoulders)

Big 21's

As you can see, we lifted three times a week and in between that we ran. Tuesday and Thursday were set aside for field work drills and fun runs. Let's be honest for a moment, nothing about these was fun. We just had to do them. I was determined to do whatever it took to get onto the field.

Here are three things that helped me persevere during my playing days:

10 LESSONS TO BECOMING A PREMIER ATHLETE

1. **Inner Circle.** My inner circle was huge in persevering during my playing years as well as dealing with injuries. When you are down and out, you really get to know who is in your corner and who is not. Whether that is family or friends, it's always great to know who you can talk to or get advice from when dealing with the struggle of being injured during football or whatever it may be. My inner circle gives advice and opinions and I can either take it or leave it.

2. **Mindset.** Having a clear understanding of what I wanted to accomplish during my playing time helped me with my mindset. I had to clear my mind of all of the noise of being injured and look ahead to playing again. If you focus only on the negative it will drag you down so much that there would never be a chance to come out of the self destruction coma. I could have looked at my injury as a failure, but in my mind it was more of a growth timeline. What am I going to do to get myself out of this situation and back on track to what I wanted to accomplish? Was I going

to continue to mope on down to the training room and complain about not getting better or was I going to take a walk on down with a bit of positivity to progress towards success.

3. **Positivity.** Being positive was the only way to get through this. It was a real struggle to wake up for weeks on end and know that I wasn't going to be able to practice or even dress out for games. I had to take this one day at a time and build on the progress of getting healthier. This didn't last for a couple of weeks, it lasted for darn near a year. Some thoughts that went through my mind during this time were:

- "Once I get healthy I will get back to playing."

- "I know therapy can be a struggle at times, but I can stay the course and return to doing the things I want to in no time."

- "Now that I am done with rehab, this whole getting back in shape is going to be fun."

- "I know I've put on a bit of weight without being as active as before, but with the right plan I'll be back to my playing weight in no time."

You might have had some of these thoughts as well along whatever journey you have struggled with as well. But I do know that if you can take these three lessons and plug them in, you will find success no matter what.

Meet Emanuel Hall

Emanuel Hall was a 6'3 170lbs Junior Wide Receiver from Centennial High School in Franklin TN. He was a standout player on the team who had a season ending injury. He was talked from behind on a play and ended up breaking his ankle. That is where I met him. The doctors had just completed a surgical repair of his ankle then shortly after that he started physical therapy. He put in the work each and every day to get stronger and to increase his range of motion throughout the joint in order for him to bounce back as an even better athlete. Emanuel took the next several weeks to finish up his physical therapy before we started working together. Upon his first session with me we focused on his goals and objectives that he wanted to accomplish while working with me. Our first order of business was to focus on ways to increase his caloric intake, so he could gain weight over the next several months. Here is a bit of what that looked like for him:

BASICS:

- 50% Carbohydrates, 30% Protein, 20% Fat

- Total daily caloric intake: 3425-3800 – calories/day (Based on RMR and Activity)

- Eat frequent meals every 2-3 hours

- Goal for Protein intake – 256-285grams/day

- Goal for Carbohydrate intake: 428-475 grams/day

- Goal for Fat intake: 76-84 grams/day

- PRE and POST workout meal consumption

10 LESSONS TO BECOMING A PREMIER ATHLETE

- o PRE – 4:1 ratio of Carbs/Protein. Ex. Power Bar or Cliff Bar with Sports Drink

- o POST – at least 45 minutes after finishing workout. Ex. Protein Drink (WHEY) with Fruit

- **Water Intake:**

- o Before exercise, consume 10-20 oz of water

- o At least 2 hours before exercise, drink about 16 oz. of fluid

- o After exercise, consume about 16-24 oz. of fluid for every pound of body weight lost during exercise

- **Additional Comments:**

- o Be sure to eat every 2-3 hours

- o Goal is to drink 64+ ounces of water per day

○ Pack your lunches for school to ensure adequate caloric intake daily

▪ Fast Snack ideas: Pretzels, Bagel w/peanut butter, trail mix w/ granola and raisins, walnuts, almonds.

6:15 am BREAKFAST – (463 calories: 59g CHO/31g PRO/11g Fat)

¾ cup of Egg Whites, ½ cup of Blueberries and Strawberries, 4 pieces of turkey bacon, ¾ cup oats

Water – (16-20 oz.)

7:30 am SCHOOL STARTS

9:00 am SNACK – (309 calories: 26g CHO/20g Protein/15g Fat)

6oz Chobani (Greek) Yogurt, 1oz of dried almonds (approximately 22)
Water – (16-20 oz.)

11:30 am LUNCH – (783 calories: 72g CHO/ 77g Protein/ 22g Fat)

> 4-6 oz. Chicken (grilled), 2 slices of wheat bread, 2 cups of green beans, ½ cup of sweet potatoes

1:30 pm SNACK /PreWorkout – (455 calories: 72g CHO/22g Protein/10g Fat)

> 1 Turkey sandwich – 2 slices of bread, 6 pieces of turkey, lettuce, and lite mayo
> 1 Large apple
> 1 oz of String Cheese
> Water (16-20 oz.)

Or

(519 calories: 72g CHO, 49 g Protein, 6g Fat)

Smoothie:

> 1 cup of 2% Milk
> 1 medium banana
> ½ cup of blueberries
> ¼ cup of raspberries
> ½ cups of strawberries
> ¼ cup of frozen vanilla yogurt

2 oz. of pineapple juice

2 scoops of Protein

3:30pm-4:30pm Workout

5:00pm – Post Workout – (Needs to be consumed within 30-45 minutes of completing the workout) (410 calories: 62g CHO, 32g Protein, 6g Fat)

1 Scoop of Protein

8 oz. of 2% Milk

1 Medium Sized Banana

7:00pm – Dinner – (548 calories: 43g CHO, 76g Protein, 9g Fat)

1 dinner roll

½ cup of brown rice

12 oz. of tilapia

1 cup of asparagus

9:30pm Snack – (519 calories: 72g CHO, 49 g Protein, 6g Fat)

Smoothie:

1 cup of 2% Milk

1 medium banana

½ cup of blueberries

¼ cup of raspberries

½ cups of strawberries

¼ cup of frozen vanilla yogurt

2 oz. of pineapple juice

2 scoops of Protein

Since this was all kind of new to him it took quite a bit of practice to start hitting enough calories per day. After we dialed in his nutrition we went over the initial evaluation where we wanted to see his strengths and weaknesses before I wrote out his programming. He was obviously a bit weaker on his injured side, but we got straight to work. Our main goal during the strength training phase was to put on mass and get as strong as possible while going into his senior year of high school at Centennial. We focused on bench press, squats, deadlifts, and last but not least: arms. This was some of the meat and potatoes of the workouts, but we wanted to be sure we could add the mass and stay injury free. That's exactly what we did. While working out, we added about 20lbs of muscle and a ton of strength and it wasn't going unnoticed. Most of his teammates were asking him where he had been training and what he was doing to get so big. It was a bit of a secret for a while due to the tremendous amount of results that were showing now. He was also getting recruited by some big schools before his injury, during, and even some after he had healed up. Some included: Cincinnati, Iowa State, Kansas, Kentucky, Louisville, Middle Tennessee State, Mississippi State, Ole Miss, UAB, and Vanderbilt. During his senior year he definitely had to make his mind up on where he was headed, but he had to take care of business on the field during this time as well. He had one more year left to make a push to his dream school. Emanuel's senior season included 47 receptions for 889 yards and 12 touchdowns as a 3 Star recruit. This definitely put him on the map. As it was coming down to the signing day process he had a ton of options to choose from, but he ended up going with Missouri and he became a tiger. This was an accomplishment in and of itself. He got hurt, rehabbed his injury and persevered to gain that college scholarship he has always wanted.

Maybe you have a similar story to Emanuel and you wish to take a similar approach. When things get tough and you have setbacks, you have to persevere and move forward to accomplish all that life has to offer you.

CHAPTER 4

DETERMINATION,
noun: firmness of
purpose; resoluteness

It took a certain level of determination to make it to the level of collegiate sports, but also to complete the task at hand. Every day was a day of tasks to be completed:

10 LESSONS TO BECOMING A PREMIER ATHLETE

1. Wake Up

2. Get Dressed

3. Walk to Workouts

4. Workout

5. Eat Breakfast

6. Class

7. Practice

8. Dinner

9. Homework/Tutoring

10. Free Time

Not always in this particular order, but this is how my days looked. From start to finish I was on a schedule. Workouts and eating were always on there, so those things were never an issue. Some things were interchangeable! A mindset of determination was inevitable or else you were going to pay the consequences of not completing these tasks. Either you left on time or else you didn't eat. You got up on time or else other players came knocking on your door. Tutoring was going to be completed or else the homework wasn't going to be done. Missed tasks = Setbacks.

With all things set forth I was determined to play offensive line, because this was the position I was recruited for. Well that took a different turn after my first year. I wanted to play any way I could, so instead of making excuses I made the jump to the defensive line. I got hurt year 1 and it just didn't go my way. I made my way back and wanted to make an impact in some sort of fashion, so d-line was where it was going to happen. It was new to me. I only played minimal snaps in high school, so learning a new position was a work in progress to say the least. New techniques, hand placements, body placement, and ways to line up across from offensive lineman was interesting to say the least. I was determined to make the best of my time, effort, and energy while making the switch to defense. Here are a few lessons I learned along the way.

1. **Never Give Up.** There are times that you can get humbled because you think you know what's right, but God had other plans. Maybe

I wasn't ever supposed to be on the offensive line to begin with. I came in playing center and left playing defensive tackle. By using my never give up attitude I was bound to fall in line somewhere and make an impact. I could have easily given up, but things in life don't come easy. Never giving up will lead to a life of happiness and fulfillment. Giving up hurts the most.

2. **Silence the "You Can't" Chatter.** There are always a ton of naysayers and those who want you to fail. I call them the You Cantters! It is technically not a word but it's the truth. They always want to bring you down and tell you that you can't be successful. Or they want to lay out all of the negative that is associated with what you are working to accomplish. I had both of these kinds of You Cantters naysaying me while I was playing football and while I was starting out in business as well. I'm not sure how most people handle this, but I had goals I wanted to accomplish so I wrote them down. Then I wrote down the steps to reach each and every one of these goals. This

helped block out all of the noise and the You Can't Chatter. It became more of You Can and things started to work in my favor. Shut them out and make goals and break down the steps to be successful and the rest will work itself out.

3. **Saying "NO."** What do I mean by this? In order to stay on a determined route to get things accomplished you have to say NO to a lot of things. I had to say no to hanging out with friends after work in high school because my plan was to work at Hillwood Country Club all day then go to Golds Gym and work out, then go home. I did this 4–5 times per week. After a few weeks people got the hint. I wasn't hanging out with folks until the weekend. It was my goal to get in shape and nothing was going to stop me. By saying NO to all of the noise, I was able to focus on getting to school and completing the run test and lift test. I wasn't always great, but by saying NO a lot, I was able to get on campus and be the only offensive lineman to accomplish/complete both of these tasks. On the flip side, by saying

NO to all of the Instagram and Facebook influencers that claim they can help you with your business, I was able to focus and find someone with a ton of credibility to help build my business. I said NO to a ton of these before I found a great fit. By doing so, I was able to focus and think about what I really wanted to achieve with my business. I said NO to friends' advice because they had never run a business before. I said NO to some family as well due to the fact that I wasn't really keen on their ideas on how I needed to build my business. With all of this I felt as if I put a lot on the back burner on the front end, but if I would have done all of this initially there is no telling where things would have ended up. Probably No Football and never becoming an entrepreneur. Sometimes NO will turn into YES later on down the road. Take Action, Stay Determined, Say NO a lot and it will all work out.

Meet Zach Polisky

Zach Polisky was a high school senior at Franklin and was looking to make it to college to play football. His story probably can resonate with a ton of people. He was determined to finish up his senior year and roll right into that college scholarship. That was all cut short when he was mid way through the season and he broke his collarbone going in for a tackle. Zach could have given up what he really wanted to accomplish in life—a college scholarship. There were ups and downs during this process. He was completely done with his senior year of football. What was he going to do next? Give up? Find a new route? No, he was determined to find a way to play at the next level for football.

Zach's mom contacted me to start some training since his next door neighbor was a coworker of mine. Day 1, we went through the initial evaluation to see what he could and could not do in regards to lifting since he wasn't too far out from his collarbone recovery. We got our 3 rep max for bench press, squat, and hang clean within the first week so we could have some good baseline measurements for training. Some of these numbers were a bit lower since he had not lifted in about 6 months due to the injury.

With the effort and energy that Zach put into each and every workout, he was determined to make the team. This wasn't any old walk on attempt. He was going to walk on at the University of Tennessee. Wow! When I heard this I was shocked. A guy who was coming off a significant injury was going to sacrifice it all to walk on at a Power 5 team. He came in three times a week and even made more attempts to work out on his own to keep his conditioning up. We trained all off season and it was getting closer and closer to the tryout day.

Our numbers from day one had significantly improved:

Broad Jump: 9'10" → 10'1"

1 RM Bench Press: 205lbs → 290lbs

1 RM Squat: 290lbsl → 425lbs

1 RM Hang Clean:225lbs→ 260lbs

As you can see, if you put the work in, the results will follow. Zach was fired up and ready to go, but had one thing left to accomplish: Make the Team. He was competing against a ton of other guys who had played in high school just like him, but there were slim pickings for who they were going to keep. Tryouts came and went. Although the tryout workout didn't go like he wanted to, it was back to the drawing board. A never-give-up attitude and determination like no one I have seen, led to Zach going to another tryout months later.

I remember Zach sending me a text asking me if he should try out again. My response was, "Why not? You have nothing to lose." So, back to the workouts and trying to stay in shape the best he could while still taking classes and doing things that college kids do. I think we had about two months to prepare. It wasn't exactly the same since he was in Knoxville and I was in Brentwood.

The second round of tryouts were closing in and I couldn't wait to hear what the results were. On the second round of tryouts he had out worked all of the other guys who were in the same position and Zach made the team. Was it the workouts? Or was it the conditioning that helped? Both might have played a little part, but really it was the determination of a kid who missed out on most of his senior season for football to prove people wrong that he could play at the next level. He made a point and he is the only kid I have worked with in 10 years who stayed the course even though the first result wasn't the best. Be like Zach and be determined in anything you do and never give up until you reach your goals in life.

CHAPTER 5

ADJUSTMENT, noun:
a small alteration or
movement made to
achieve a desired fit,
appearance, or result

Making adjustments in my playing time helped me become a better person and teammate. All I wanted to do was help the team. Because of that, I made the switch to the defensive line. It was tough, as it was something completely new for me. From it I learned that being able to adjust to new things will only help you down the road. You can't limit yourself in order to succeed.

As the defensive side of the ball was a bit more challenging, I wouldn't have changed this. Lots of extra running, getting yelled at, and actually getting the heck knocked out of me, so there was no turning back now. I had to make the adjustments and determine if this was going to be the best spot for me to help the team win.

As time passed and workouts/practice came and went, it was finally time for the spring scrimmage. It was coming soon enough whether I wanted it to or not. I had to suck it up and try and achieve what I had set forth to accomplish: a starting position. As this was a new thing to me, making this adjustment taught me a few things. Below are three things that I learned while I made this transition.

1. **Take things in stride.** It can get frustrating learning a new position, but I took it one day at a time. If I did this, there was going to be more room for improvement. Getting frustrated would have made things a bit more difficult and more challenging. Just like with a

new exercise program, you have to take it in stride because it's NEW.

2. **Be patient.** Since this was a position that I had never played, having patience was only going to help me in the long run. I knew I wasn't going to start with the 1's because I hadn't had enough experience. Once I learned the play book, I knew it was only a matter of time before I was in the rotation. It paid off because during the first scrimmage after the change of position, I was in the rotation with the starters. If you are patient and stick to the plan, anything is possible.

3. **You can always overcome change.** There are always choices we make that lead us down a certain path and we can choose to overcome those choices or play the victim. I chose to overcome those things. I wanted to prove to myself that I could play on the other side of the ball even though I hadn't played defense since high school. With the right plan and attitude you can do anything. Adjustments come and go in life, and how you handle these things will determine your long-term success.

Meet Natalie Vannoy

When Natalie started at Premier Performance Training she was an elite high school swimmer who seemed to have a busier schedule than I did. She would go to school, then swim practice, then go work out, and finally do homework. It was a tough go of things for any high school kid, but she knew what she had to do in order to make it to the next level for swimming.

Coming from her club swim team I figured she already knew how to work out and what all a training program entailed. I was wrong. She knew things about working out, but had not been on a real structured training program. This was definitely an adjustment for her. How so? Well, yes, she was a great athlete who had done a ton of swim training and practice over the years. Heck, she had even done a lot of bodyweight dry land training. However, she had never done anything as structured as a full on 2–3 times per week strength training workout program.

While it was new to her, it wasn't anything she couldn't handle. We sat down, went over her goals and got to work. My number one priority was for her to work out at a high level and stay injury free. Why? If my work in the weight room was to destroy every athlete I came in contact with, I would be out of a job.

Natalie put in her time in the pool and for her dry land training and landed an awesome swimming scholarship at Queens University. It's one of the top (if not the best) Division 2 swimming programs. That was a huge accomplishment for her.

All of the adjustments she had made for her senior year were paying off in a big way. She continued training with us in the off season as well. During the COVID-19 pandemic, Natalie made many adjustments with her sport and has stuck with it. She got her swimming in at her neighbors house while things were shut down and even drove 30 minutes to train with Coach Aaron in order to stay on track with her goals. She finished off by far one of the best accomplishments by one of our athletes. She placed sixth at Nationals in the 50-meter Freestyle, first in the 200-meter Freestyle Medley, and she was a part of the Division 2 National Championship for Women's Swimming at Queens in 2021.

If you can't make adjustments to your schedule or your life, you might not ever be able to accomplish things you didn't think were possible. Anything is possible!

CHAPTER 6

> ACHIEVEMENT, noun:
> a thing done successfully,
> typically by effort,
> courage, or skill

I achieved what I had set forth to achieve back during my senior year of high school. Go to college and play at the next level. It didn't matter at the time where that was. I just wanted to do so.

10 LESSONS TO BECOMING A PREMIER ATHLETE

I made it to Lambuth. I came into the spring as a second-third string rotation for defense and I was okay with that. I had spent the previous year recovering from my injury, sitting on the sidelines, wishing and waiting time and time again with nothing. I would say that achievement isn't always what the coaches think it should be, but what you find. It was tough enough to get to that second-string rotation considering the obstacles I had encountered and I was proud of what I had accomplished coming off of an injury. Second-third string rotation was a victory at the time.

Then came the scrimmage! I did well, but not great. I had a few assists with tackles, but nothing outstanding. Spring ball had wrapped up and things were looking promising for me going into the next year. I committed to defense and decided it was a great fit after all. I had at least three more years of eligibility since I had redshirted my first year. It was time to reflect on how I was going to move forward at Lambuth University.

Here are three things that I learned while achieving my dream of playing collegiate football:

1. **Don't let others try and talk you out of chasing your dreams.** There are always those who don't want you to succeed. They want you to be just like them—average. I wasn't trying to be average, I wanted to be successful and make a name for myself. There will be those in your ear trying to talk you out of every decision you make, but at the end of the day it's up to you to succeed in life. Want what others don't. Be weird and do great things.

2. **When the going gets tough, don't quit!** Things were not easy trying to play college sports. I don't care what others might tell you. It's very regimented and things are done on a schedule. That was a big change for me. My injury happened and I could have quit right then and there, but I didn't want to be remembered as a quitter. I persevered and achieved what I wanted to accomplish. I came from a small high school with only one football offer to play college sports and I did. Mission Accomplished!

3. **Exceed your own expectations.** I set a goal to go to college and play football. I did that and

exceeded what I thought I could do. I went in as an offensive lineman and left playing the defensive side of the ball. I didn't know it was possible, so that's a WIN.

Meet Bryan Rice

I met Bryan Rice via a brief introduction to his mom, who worked at a local physical therapy clinic. I was there to speak to the clinic director, but I ended up getting a client out of it, which was a win win. Bryan was a part of the Ravenwood football team and played defensive end. It took a few weeks to get him into the facility because at the time he was still in season for football. I believe it was his sophomore year. Once the season was over, it was time to train.

One of the first things I do when athletes come into the facility is ask them how much they squat, bench, and hang clean, sometimes dead lift. Bryan without hesitation stated that he squatted 405 pounds. I looked at him with a bit of a grin and said, "Prove it." I like kids who have a ton of confidence, but I want to be sure they are not giving me any fluff. So, we warmed up and got to work with him proving his 405-

pound squat. It didn't go as planned, but he did give a valiant effort.

Bryan is a guy who no matter what you throw at him he always goes above and beyond. He was determined to be great and achieve things that people said were impossible. He worked his way through the off season and became a force to be reckoned with at the defensive end spot at Ravenwood. He went on to win the Defensive Player of the Year award in Williamson County his junior year. His junior year he played so great that during his senior year, teams double- and triple-teamed him on just about every single play. He fought hard and battled through some minor aches and pains to help his team make it to the TSSAA State Championship in 6A. Even though the final wasn't the outcome he was looking for, he had achieved a lot in those short few years.

Bryan could have relaxed after all of that, but he wanted to accomplish more. Bryan went on to wrestle after football season his senior year and was the only person that year and maybe ever at Ravenwood to go to the state tournament in wrestling. Achieving things that people didn't think possible was the name of the game for Bryan.

Tons of hard work played a huge part in Bryan achieving greatness in football and wrestling in high school. Proving the doubters wrong and making a statement for how good of an athlete he was wasn't easy.

Bryan is now at Shorter University fulfilling his dream of playing college football. He wanted to challenge himself to play football at the next level. Being a star at the high school level seemed as if it came easy for Bryan, but he doesn't settle for being good, he wants to be great!

CHAPTER 7

REFLECTION, noun:
serious thought or
consideration

After my knee injury in my sophomore year, not only did I have to reflect on continuing my football career, but also my education. I went from a Computer Science major to History to Athletic Training or whatever their equivalent was. I knew I didn't want to pursue computer science after one class, as I was unable to understand the professor. Then there was history—the degree where you make no money. Athletic Training or the equivalent I knew I would enjoy because I was always in the weight room, so much so that it felt like home.

Monitoring the weight room was also my work study in school, so I was there all the time. I enjoyed it because I could work out whenever I wanted to. After year two, I was going to continue to play football or go to another school where they had the degree I wanted. I spent plenty of time reflecting on leaving friends I had made over the past few years, leaving football for good, and doing something completely different with my studies. It was a tough choice, but at the end of the day I knew I wasn't going any further than Lambuth University to play football. Coach Vic Wallace always told me I was too small to play or start, so I knew the best option was to move on and create the next chapter of my life. Once my mind was made up, I ended up taking a walk to the coaches office to have a chat with Coach.

1. **Make a decision and stick with it.** I had to decide on whether I was going to get a degree just because, or move to a school that had

exactly what I wanted to do with my career and life. This wasn't an easy decision at all. Trust me, there was a ton of contemplation that happened because I was not 100% clear on what I wanted to do. A lot of times we have these same thoughts with our health and fitness. Do you jump back and forth between exercise programs or nutrition plans, or do you stay the course just because it's a steady schedule? It can be tough, but at the end of it all, a bit of time and reflection is all that you need to make the best decision.

2. **Go with your gut.** I had a ton of mixed feelings about leaving the team and pursuing other things besides football, but I couldn't have been happier with my decision. I made up my mind and marched to the coaches office and let them know my thoughts on leaving. It was a tough decision. I was leaving a program that I had been a part of for two years and I had met some pretty amazing people during that time. My gut told me to walk away, and that's what I did. I definitely wouldn't be in the spot I am today if it weren't for that gut decision.

3. **When one door closes another one opens.**
   The football door was closing, but I was
   marching onward to another door swinging
   wide open. I was about to run through it and
   pursue a degree I was passionate about:
   Health and Human Performance with an
   Exercise Science concentration. You never
   know what opportunities are available to you
   until you make those tough choices in life. I
   walked away from what I thought was my
   passion in life, but I was wrong.

Meet Anders Mount

Anders Mount was a football player at Brentwood
High School whose main goal was to start for his team
his senior year. He stood about 6'3" and about 200
pounds. He had mainly played on the offensive line
the last three years, but was up for any position at this
point. He just wanted to play.

Anders spent a ton of time reflecting on how it felt to
be the tiny offensive lineman and sat most of the time
he had invested in his sport on the sideline. We
chatted frequently about how it made him feel and

how he was going to prove to his coaches and teammates that he deserved to be the number one guy. After our initial conversation, Anders began training with me 2–3 times per week. Sometimes it was in the evening and other times we met before school. He was consistent, did what he was supposed to, and started to make a ton of progress.

With some time working together, Anders gained about 25 pounds and was getting faster. Then he went to a yoga class, where he had a bit of a setback. He strained/pulled a muscle in his hamstring, which caused him pain and discomfort. We tried to work around it and even added in some exercises and movements that would help strengthen his hips and glutes to make a better comeback after a minor setback. Yet, he was frustrated. He couldn't lift what he used to lift due to his physical restrictions while he recovered, and we weren't able to work at his speed. These limitations were the death of the progress we were trying to make.

Anders ended up having to get PRP injections and let his hamstring heal for about 6–8 weeks. Once that was all cleared up and ready to rock, we got back to it. We were steadily gaining ground before spring practice was about to kick off. Anders was gaining weight, increasing his strength, and looking more and more like a high school starter every day. The season started and Anders had put in the work to be exactly where he needed to be in order to be in the rotation on Day 1. Anders was about 6'3" and had gained 40 pounds to be at about 245 pounds his senior year.

His time came and it was well worth the wait. He had made such an impression during the game that the opponents were asking why he hadn't started the entire year. It didn't matter to him as much, because he knew he had taken the time months ago to reflect on his senior year and what he wanted to accomplish. He had done just that and even more.

CHAPTER 8

BOLD, adjective:
(of a person, action,
or idea) showing an
ability to take risks;
confident and
courageous

I took bold action to march my happy self down to the coaches' office because I wanted to let them know my displeasure around scholarship money and a few other things. I was pleasant, but wanted to get my point across. I thought that I had earned a bit more money towards school and football, but I guess Coach had other plans. I made my case and I told him thank you for allowing me to come to the university to play, but my time here was done and I was moving on. I knew it was the right move for me, especially as I wasn't sticking around to bust my tail in order for him to award those who didn't even show up half the time. Onward and upward I went. I was done and not too upset about it. Although, I wish I had taken my helmet and my jersey, but I suppose you don't think of everything while you are on your way out.

Here are three things I learned about being bold with my decision making.

1. **Don't be afraid of the response.** I told my coach that I wasn't going to come back for my junior year and he made it sound like it was the worst decision ever. He said that my dad had written him a letter saying what a big mistake he was going to make by letting me walk. That was a lie. My dad never wrote a letter or would have never thought of doing so. I felt like my coach was trying to make me feel bad for telling him my decision to walk. At that time I was so upset that it didn't really matter what he said, I wasn't coming back.

Sometimes the response to our bold actions is unexpected, but it helps us grow as human beings into bigger and better people.

2. **Taking a risk without much reward.** I took the risk of leaving the team and headed to a new school without knowing what I had gotten myself into. I was hoping to leave and then graduate on time, but the registrar had other plans. I had lost approximately 20 or so credit hours along the way on transferring, and there was no way in heck I was going to be able to make these up in a timely manner. It ended up taking me an extra year to finish my degree, but it was worth it. Not every risk we take ends up the way we want. It's how we respond to it that makes us who we are in the end.

3. **Great friends last forever.** Even though I was leaving some of the greatest friends I could have asked for in the past two years, they still stuck with me when I left. We still went to each other's family's houses, we were even in each other's weddings, and we were there when we needed each other. I couldn't have

asked for a better group of friends to hang out with on a consistent basis.

Meet Tyrese Cox

Tyrese Cox was a football player from Tullahoma, TN, which is about 90 minutes from where I was training in Williamson County. He was a tall (6'3"), 185-pound defensive end who was a bit lanky, but wasn't afraid of anyone on or off the field. Ty was a freshman/sophomore when he began working out with Eli Grow. Eli was another teammate of Ty's who I had previously worked with.

Ty noticed Eli's work ethic and growth and wanted to come to where Eli was training because he had hopes and dreams of playing collegiate football. So, Ty began training with me after his junior year making the drive from Tullahoma 1–2 times each week for training. He was determined to go somewhere for football. He didn't really care where, he just wanted to go.

It was a bold move for Ty to drive almost 3 hours round trip to train with a guy who was working with some of the best area high school football athletes. Some folks couldn't believe it, but he knew it was his way out of Tullahoma. He needed this for him. He stepped outside of his comfort zone and made a long trip each and every week to chase a dream of playing football in college.

Ty's senior year he wrapped up all kinds of accomplishments, including anchoring one of the best defenses in Tullahoma history, 91 tackles with 24 of those for loss. He was also named to the 4-A All State team. After his senior year he signed to play with Tennessee Tech for the next four years.

Not only was it a bold move to travel miles away for training, but even bigger and bolder, he turned down some smaller schools to chase his dream of playing Division 1 football. That's exactly what he did.

CHAPTER 9

OVERCOME, verb:
succeed in dealing
with (a problem or
difficulty)

To overcome an injury was one of the hardest things
I had ever done up to as a young collegiate athlete. To
get to that point, I had worked a ton of hard jobs and
done some challenging things, but an injury that had
me sidelined for almost a year was terrible.

THE ATHLETIC ADVANTAGE

I sustained the injury during practice when going through a pass set drill. I planted my right leg back and all of a sudden it buckled. I didn't think much of it at the time, but as soon as I realized what happened I immediately got a real uncomfortable feeling on the front of my knee cap. I tried to walk it off, but the pain was throbbing. Practice for me that day ended early as I was headed to the training room to get it checked out.

We didn't have a physical therapist, only an athletic trainer named Jason. He looked at it and did a few tests, but it seemed to make it a bit worse after he had worked on it. Off I went back to my fourth floor room with only stairs ahead of me. It took me a long time to get up to my room, but I knew I wasn't going to complain about a ton.

Weeks went by and I had to go to the local doctor in Martin, TN, to get it checked out. Lots of other tests and twists and such. The conclusion was an imbalance in my quadricep and hamstring. One was stronger than the other and this led to the collapse of my knee that day at practice. I had a game plan now and I was off to get this knee healed and back on the field.

Here are the three things that I learned from this long drawn out experience...

1. **Things don't always go as planned.** I was amped up to be a freshman with an equal chance to make the travel team, but my injury came at probably the worst time. It was during camp and that hope of making the travel team was cut short. If it weren't for the knee injury I probably would have stayed on the offensive side of the ball. My injury led to an opportunity to take control, get healthy, and possibly find a new spot on the team.

2. **Ask for help.** Because I was an athlete, I didn't want to ask for help when I could barely walk around campus. Boy, that was a huge mistake. It took more energy to do it all myself instead of letting others help me or even asking for a bit of help with my books, cafeteria tray, etc. Asking for help isn't a bad thing. It shows that you are human and want others to be there for you. That goes for anything: after an injury, if you don't understand the playbook, or if you can't

perform a lift properly. Asking will solve a ton more problems than sitting back quietly.

3. **Don't rush the process.** The process was long and I thought at times that I wouldn't recover from this injury. I was hoping that it would take about 2–3 weeks and I would be back on the field. I kept checking back in with Jason and doing my exercises, but the pain was still there. I focused on lifting on my own as well to try and stay in shape the best I could. I found that being patient, doing my exercises in my dorm room, and doing water aerobic therapy was going to be the best plan for me. Rushing back was in the front of my mind because I missed being in a routine with my teammates, but little did I know that it would take almost a year to make a full recovery.

Be Patient → Don't Rush the Process → Recovery Happens with Time

Meet Josh Phillips

Josh Phillips was a junior golfer from middle Tennessee who had been working with Premier Performance Training since he was in seventh grade. He worked his way up the rankings and was going into his eighth grade season at Page Middle School to do something that had never been done before at his school: win a Middle School Golf Championship. Josh trained 2–3 times per week minimum or whenever he didn't have a tournament or a school golf meet. We worked on flexibility, mobility, and strength training during our sessions.

Josh continued to progress with his training, and the Middle School golf season of his eighth grade year began. His season went well and the final tournament of the year approached. Who was going to win and be the next middle school champion in Williamson County?

The day of the final tournament, the team was fired up. The competition was close. It came down to the last day with a very small margin for error.

At the end of it all, Josh and his teammates came out victorious. They had accomplished so much during this season. A first championship banner for Page Middle School.

After that season, Josh was back at it. He was on the course practicing and in the weight room getting stronger and working on his flexibility and mobility. A few months into the off season, he told me that he was moving due to his dad getting a new job. I was a bit in shock, but knew he could win wherever he was going.

Josh and his family headed up to New Hampshire to settle in. Josh searched for new golf coaches to help with his swing and overall mechanics as a golfer. We switched to an all online approach to training since the move. We met three times a week via Facetime to work on the same things we focused on while he was in Tennessee.

We were 3–4 months into our training sessions, when he was practicing at a golf course, and all of a sudden he experienced a tightness in his chest. It was hard to swing a golf club due to what we thought was a minor pulled muscle or some tightness. This wasn't a good sign! Tightness on a downswing.

10 LESSONS TO BECOMING A PREMIER ATHLETE

His chest was painful, and it was going to take some time to get his injury figured out. He was going to have to overcome a weird injury like I did in order to make a push for the New Hampshire High School State Championship in golf. I started reaching out to Physical Therapy clinics in the area where he lived and I stumbled upon Mike Boyle's place, which was closer to Boston.

If you don't know who Mike Boyle is, look him up. He's a strength and conditioning mastermind. His Physical Therapist took Josh in and immediately got to work on his problem. Recovery was challenging, but we knew what the issue was now since it was diagnosed, which meant we had a plan to overcome it. Josh went to therapy 1–2 times a week and worked on his stretches at home to make the recovery process.

Once he had a diagnosis, a plan, and was healing properly, we got back to it with our Facetime workouts.

A few weeks later Josh became the New Hampshire High School State Champion as a sophomore. Injuries stink, but it's how you respond to them that will make or break you.

CHAPTER 10

FINISH, noun:
to come to an end

My days of playing college football were winding to a close. I had informed the coaches that I would not be returning to the team the following year, but I always wanted to finish anything that I started. Even though it was tough to continue going to practice and participating in drills, I knew I had to do what was right. Show up, practice, and be on the team until it was time to transfer. I was looking forward to moving even before the off season was over. It was hard to focus and not think about the endless possibilities that were ahead for me.

Below are three things I learned from my playing days coming to an end.

1. **Finish what you started.** I've never been one to quit on something or quit before my time was done. That's why I committed to staying on the team and finishing practices, study hall time, and even workouts with the team, even though I knew I wasn't coming back next season. I never want to be remembered as the guy who left his teammates high and dry. My dad always said, "If you start something, you better be able to finish it." That's what I did. I left school knowing that I had done everything possible to give it my all.

2. **Share the positive no matter how you feel.** I use my positive experiences from my playing days to tell stories to the athletes that I now train. Maybe they can relate and maybe not,

but I do know what it takes to get to the next level of college sports. Although my playing time was short, I tell these stories of how the experience shaped and molded me into the person I am today. The kids enjoy these and although they won't admit it, I am usually correct when it comes to the strenuous schedule that athletes endure on a daily basis.

3. **Be respectful to your coaches.** Being respectful isn't a hard thing to do, but you would be surprised how many folks leave a program and just talk bad about their coaches. I tried to be as respectful as possible even though I didn't agree with all of their decisions. My thoughts are that you don't even know who you might need a recommendation from or a job from 5–10 years from now. Since leaving Lambuth I have come in contact with former players and even coaches who have lent a hand or helped out when I needed it the most.

10 LESSONS TO BECOMING A PREMIER ATHLETE

Meet Eli Grow

Let's take a trip back almost to 2016, when I came in contact with a young man named Eli Grow. For some of you this name may ring a bell and for others you may have no idea who I am talking about.

Eli was a junior at Tullahoma High School, which is roughly 75 minutes south of Franklin, TN. He played quarterback for the school and was well liked by darn near everyone. His mom was operating a heck of a gelato business and his dad ran the family environmental business.

Everyone always commented that Eli was always smiling and always wanted to help others. No matter the day or time, Eli was grinning from ear to ear. You could have told him to run six laps as fast as he could, but he always had that grin on his face no matter how much pain he was in. He worked his tail off in the weight room day in and day out. He would come to the facility and train 1–2 times a week, but he was also dedicated to working out on his own at the school. He was in the weight room all the time. All the time. I darn near think the coaches gave him a key to the gym because they were tired of him asking if he could come workout.

Eli wanted to be the best and there wasn't anyone who was going to stop him. He texted me daily asking questions about his workout program and if there was anything extra he could do at home to get better. You can't teach that burning desire, you have to want it. He worked on improving his lifts. He worked on his footwork. He worked on his agility and speed. There wasn't a day that went by that I didn't receive a text message asking how to do something or if that was all he was supposed to do that day.

Eli wanted that Collegiate Scholarship more than any kid I have ever trained. He knew he was a bit undersized for a quarterback, but he wasn't going to let that stop him from pursuing his dream.

Coming around to his senior year, Eli was getting looks from a few smaller schools in the area, but the one that caught his eye was Mississippi College. Eli was happier than a pig in mud, smiling from ear to ear, when he told me, "I've decided to play college football at Mississippi College." I knew he was pumped. He had gone on a college visit and fallen in love with the school.

> Fellas,
>
> Welcome to the MC Football Program.
> I have attached a workout that you guys can start ASAP. This will get through our spring game. At which time we will have a demonstration session showing you guys several lifts and explain how we expect things done when in the weight room. At this time I will give you a new packet with more details to last you through the summer.
>
> Let me know if you have any questions.
> Thanks and GO CHOCS!!!!

This was proof that he was finally accepted into the CHOCS family and now it was time to go to work for the football program. Eli came in to work out on April 30, 2016. He was pumped up. He had texted me to let me know that he was on his way and he would be on time. Sometimes it took a bit longer due to his drive time. I patiently waited as the door flung open to the gym. There he was, smiling and anticipating his workout. He put on his workout shoes and then it was time to warm up. I can't remember if we started on the treadmill or not, but we went right into some band work, then dynamic warm-up, then then some speed work.

We generally took our time. I knew that I wanted to get in as much as possible, so we chatted and worked for what felt like two hours. We finished our workout and he wanted to stick around and do a few things extra. This was normal for him. Eli wanted to do extra all the time, which was a great sign of someone who wanted it. He always wanted to finish the workout no matter how much time it took.

As we were wrapping up, I gave him a high five, which I typically do once someone is finished. Some of us are like Eli and will go the extra mile and finish everything that they start, but others want the easy way out. They want to quit, make excuses, and play the blame game.

Be like Eli and FINISH. "Never take anything for granted." —Eli Grow

CONCLUSION AND WHAT'S NEXT

There you have it, the 10 Lessons to set you apart from being a mediocre athlete and becoming a Premier Athlete.

There is not ever a clear path to becoming a great athlete. Everyone has a journey that has gotten them from point A to point B.

Some have had it easier than others, but most have gone through many stages of adversity. It's how you bounce back that will set you apart from being good to being great.

Following these 10 Lessons will help set you apart from the rest of the pack.

1. Discipline

2. Friendships

3. Perseverance

4. Determination

5. Adjustment

6. Achievement

7. Reflection

8. Bold

9. Overcome

10. Finish

You can always get better, improve where needed, and become the best athlete you can be. Trust yourself and trust the process of becoming that Premier athlete.

Made in the USA
Columbia, SC
15 May 2025

57956368R00088